Writing and Updating Technology Plans

A Guidebook with Sample Policies on CD-ROM

John M. Cohn, Ann L. Kelsey, and Keith Michael Fiels

Neal-Schuman Publishers, Inc.
New York   London

Published by Neal-Schuman Publishers, Inc.
100 Varick St.
New York, NY 10013

Printed and bound in the United States of America

Library of Congress Cataloging-in-Publication Data

Cohn, John M.
    Writing and updating technology plans : a guidebook with sample policies on
CD-ROM / John M. Cohn, Ann L. Kelsey, Keith Michael Fiels.
        p.   cm.
    Includes bibliographical references (p.   ) and index.
    ISBN 1–55570–365–8
    1. Libraries—United States—Data processing—Planning. I. Kelsey, Ann L.   II. Fiels,
Keith Michael.   III. Title.
Z678.9.A4 U623 2000
025'.00285—dc21   99–048200

Contents

Figures

Acknowledgments

The authors would like to acknowledge Paul Kissman of the Massachusetts Board of Library Commissioners, Ray Ewick and Virginia Andis of the Indiana State Library, Kathleen Bloomberg of the Illinois State Library, Sharon Brettschneider of the Connecticut State Library, Tom Sloan of the Delaware State Library, Elizabeth Breedlove of the New Jersey State Library, Carol Desch and Fredrick Smith of the New York State Library, and Elizabeth Ann Funk of the Pennsylvania State Library, who recommended many of the public library plans included in this work. The authors would like to acknowledge the work of other state agency staff who helped 6,000 public libraries develop technology plans in 1998, most for the first time.

The authors would also like to thank Linda Braun, for her assistance with the school library planning section, and Lorraine Barry and Hasmik Assidrian, who assisted in locating plans on the Web. We are most grateful to the fifty librarians who granted permission to reproduce their technology plans.

Finally, the authors acknowledge Kristine S. McCorkle of *A Way with Words and the World Wide Web* in Bel Air, Maryland, who created the Web page for this book's technology plans.

Preface: Why This Book and Why Now?

The purpose of this book and CD resource is to provide any library that is undertaking the development of a technology plan with a general introduction to the components of and process for developing a plan, while also providing specific examples of plans that illustrate a variety of approaches. These approaches include stand-alone technology plans, which are more typical in public libraries, and organizational plans with library components, which are more typical of college and university and school library plans. A number of special library plans are also included.

The book is designed to provide a general introduction to the concepts and key issues in technology planning. It outlines a general planning process, suitable for libraries of all types and all sizes, that can be used by any library to develop either a stand-alone plan or the library component of an organizational plan.

The Introduction offers a brief history of technology planning in public, school, academic, and special libraries. Chapter 1 explains what a technology plan is and what purpose it serves.

The "heart" of the guide is contained in Chapters 2–4. Chapter 2 provides an overview of the basic components of a technology plan, illustrated with numerous examples from actual plans. Chapters 3 and 4 address various aspects of the development of a plan as a chronological process, discussing methods by which the components are created and developed following an assessment of purpose and need.

Chapter 5 discusses the actual preparation and writing of the plan. Chapter 6 describes how libraries implement, evaluate, and keep their plans current. Chapter 7 considers the elements that distinguish good technology plans from those that are not quite as good. A concluding chapter reviews how to make the best use of a technology plan to further the library's goals and objectives.

The book also allows a public or school library that is preparing a technology plan as part of an application for the newly established federal E-rate program to meet the basic planning requirements under this program. (The authors note, however, that these requirements are evolving and will be subject to some change each year.)

A CD-ROM adds to the comprehensiveness of the information. It includes fifty technology plans collected from different types of libraries and a Webliography of technology planning resources available on the World Wide Web. The accompanying sample plans are organized on a CD-ROM for two reasons. First, despite the fact that many plans are becoming available on the World Wide Web, many outstanding plans are still not Web accessible, and many Web sites are in varying stages of construction and/or currency. The plans included here have all been selected based on their outstanding or unique qualities. Second, locating plans within Web sites and making one's way among sites is considerably quicker and easier in theory than it is in practice—one of the reasons librarians are not in any immediate danger of extinction! It is often difficult to determine where a plan begins or ends in a Web-based environment. The plans included in this book are easily accessible—and, of course, the URLs will not change on the CD.

A listing of relevant and recommended print and Web sources is provided at the end of most chapters. Appendix A at the end of the book also provides an overview of a number of unique Web-based resources for technology planners. A number of these resources are particularly valuable since they are specifically geared toward libraries of a particular type.

Introduction

A Brief History of Library Technology Planning

PUBLIC LIBRARIES

Traditionally, public library planning has focused on the process of developing an annual budget request from a town, city, county, or district. Occasionally, a major project requiring a special appropriation required the development of a multiyear project plan. During the 1970s, these projects increasingly involved the purchase of library computer systems.

The widespread development of long-range plans by public libraries began in earnest with the publication in 1980 by the American Library Association (ALA) of *A Planning Process for Public Libraries*, a work developed for the Public Library Association. In 1987, the ALA's *Planning and Role Setting for Public Libraries: A Manual of Options and Procedures*, focused more attention on the identification by the public library of priority roles within the community. Neither manual specifically mentions the word *technology*, although several of the roles in the 1987 manual were clearly consistent with the use of technology.

The newest iteration of a planning process for public libraries, *Planning for Results: A Public Library Transformation Process*, published by the Public Library Association in 1998, includes examples of how technology can support many of the priority service responses that replaced the former roles of the 1987 manual. In addition, "information literacy" is discussed as a significant service response for public libraries. In 1999, the Public Library Association issued a complementary guide to *Planning for Results* entitled *Wired for the Future: Developing Your Technology Plan.* This latter book is discussed in later chapters of the present volume.

The current growth of interest in technology planning is most directly attributable to the passage by Congress of the Telecommunications Act of 1996, which established the Universal Service Fund for schools and libraries. Under this program, first implemented in 1998–1999, schools and public libraries were eligible for significant discounts for telephone, telecommunications and Internet services, as well as the costs of telecommunications, equipment and wiring within school and public library buildings. A key component of this program was the requirement that an eligible school or public library have a technology plan.

Nearly 5,000 public libraries and library consortia submitted technology plans in 1998. In many instances, these were the first technology plans developed by the libraries. Because the law specified that a designated agency within the state—generally a department of education for schools and a state library agency for public libraries—approve each plan, many state agencies developed training materials and workshops for libraries.

Many technology plans developed by public libraries within the last few years have been specifically intended to meet the requirements of the Universal Service Discount program. One goal of this book is to help libraries to develop a plan that will meet local needs *and* incorporate elements required for participation in this program.

ACADEMIC LIBRARIES

Libraries within colleges and universities are guided by the priorities of their host institutions. Service programs and priorities for the implementation of technology are, in large measure, defined by institutional economic constraints and by the technological priorities set by the institutions.

The 1970s and 1980s were good years for the introduction of information technology in academic libraries. The period was characterized by the extensive deployment of information technology (e.g., local, integrated systems, machine-readable databases, computerized indexes) designed to streamline operations and improve services. It was only during the later 1980s and the early 1990s that budgetary pressures became severe and decision making more complicated as funding became less certain.

In today's environment, academic libraries face an array of issues that are changing the nature of higher education nationwide. These issues include the need to serve remote users who may never actually appear on campus; providing access to electronic resources while simultaneously paying for print-based materials; reconfiguring physical space to accommodate new technologies; and meeting user (student, faculty, and administration) expectations for new services in a networked environment.

These new responsibilities have resulted in an increasing emphasis on planning. As with everything else, library technology planning takes place in the context of overall institutional planning; however, writing in 1996, Kenneth C. Green, director of the Campus Computing Project, observed that

> [A] decade into what some have called the "computer revolution" in higher education, it is striking that most campuses still operate without a strategic or financial plan for information technology. . . . The number of campuses with [such] plans for technology will likely increase over the next three years . . .

The project's 1998 National Survey of Information Technology in Higher Education reported, however, that just under half of all U.S. colleges have a strategic plan for information technology.

Clearly, despite the increasing pervasiveness of computer technology on our campuses, technology plans are still not the norm among our colleges and universities. Academic librarians must nonetheless initiate their own planning processes and, if necessary, create their own plans. In so doing, they must remain cognizant of their institution's articulated mission and knowledgeable about the emerging technologies that will support the changing environment of higher education in the early 21st century. They must also be an integral part of whatever planning activity occurs on their respective campuses.

SCHOOL LIBRARIES

Many of the first plans for school library technology were developed as grant proposals for Title III of the Elementary and Secondary Education Act (ESEA), which provided federal funding for the development of school library media centers in the late 1970s and early 1980s.

During the late 1980s and 1990s, Information Power, a nationwide project of the American Association of School Libraries and the Reader's Digest Foundation, served as the basis and framework for many school library media center plans. Often, however, responsibility for technology planning was vested with district technology coordinators, and the majority of school libraries either had no plan or were not even mentioned in the district plan.

Within the last three years, two developments at the federal level have spurred planning efforts in school library media centers. The first was the reauthorization of the Library Services and Technology Act in 1997 and the second was the creation of the E-rate program in 1998.

In 1997, Congress reauthorized the Library Services and Construction Act as the Library Services and Technology Act. In the process, school libraries for the first time became eligible recipients of federal grants administered by state agencies. Since states have historically required applicants to have completed a long-range plan, this change in federal requirements has led a number of states to begin developing school library planning models and to begin providing assistance to school libraries in developing long-range plans. Most of these plans contain a technology component.

Over 20,000 school districts also submitted technology plans under the newly established E-rate telecommunications discount program in 1998–1999. While most of these plans do not include any detailed library component, most do at least mention libraries.

SPECIAL LIBRARIES

While the terms "public," "academic," and "school," conjure up neatly characterized images of specific types of libraries, the term "special" library is less easy to categorize. Special libraries may be subsets of large public or academic libraries where planning is a tradition. On the other hand, they may be part of a corporation, hospital, or museum or associated with a nonprofit group or society. In these organizations, planning within the organization generally, and the library specifically, may be historically less entrenched.

Special libraries in institutions with a strong planning culture will be more likely to have a history of long-range, strategic, and technology planning. The history within the corporate sector, however, is different. A study by James M. Matarazzo, Laurence Prusak, and Michael R. Gauthier, *Valuing Corporate Libraries: A Survey of Senior Managers,* published by the Special Libraries Association in 1990, called attention to the fact that there had been little planning by corporate libraries to deal with the significant technological and organizational changes that were sweeping the corporate world.

However, as restructuring, outsourcing, and downsizing hit the corporate library world hard in the 1990s, strategic planning became an important tool for special librarians trying to demonstrate its value to their corporations. Planning within the special library environment became a popular topic for conference programs, journal articles, and books, and it remains so. The Special Libraries Association began to publish greater numbers of books and studies on the subject, including *Strategic Planning Basics for Special Librarians* by Doris Asantewa in 1992 and *The Impact of the Special Library on Corporate Decision Making* by Joanne Gard Marshall in 1993. Robert Irving Berkman's report, *Rethinking the Corporate Information Center: A Blueprint for the 21st Century,* published in 1995 by FIND/SVP, addressed the interrelationships between technological innovations and the sweeping changes overtaking the information needs of the corporate and public sectors.

Although strategic planning remains the focus of the special library sector, formalized planning for technology, either as a component of a strategic planning process or as a stand-alone plan, is becoming more important. This is due in part to the Special Libraries Association report *Competencies for Special Librarians of the 21st Century*, edited by Barbara M. Spiegelman and published in 1997, which delineates the professional and personal competencies required of special librarians. More than one of these competencies address technology directly or indirectly. More special librarians are now developing technology plans or including technology within broader strategic plans. Articles such as Richard Hulser's "Integrating Technology into Strategic Planning," published in the February 1998 issue of *Information Outlook*, underscore the increasing value of technology planning within special libraries.

SOURCES

Asentewa, Doris. *Strategic Planning Basics for Special Libraries.* Washington, D.C.: Special Libraries Association, 1992.
This guide for developing and managing a strategic plan within the context of the special library focuses on technology and technological issues as part of the planning process culminating in the development of strategic paths.

Berkman, Robert Irving. *Rethinking the Corporate Information Center: A Blueprint for the 21st Century.* New York: FIND/SVP, 1995.
This is a detailed and complete overview of the changes, many technology driven, affecting the corporate information sector. Chapters 4 and 5 specifically address planning issues and concepts, including conducting an information needs analysis and creating an information map.

Goetsch, Lori A., ed. *Information Technology Planning.* New York: Haworth Press, 1999.
The essays in this volume, which was copublished simultaneously as *Journal of Library Administration*, vol. 26, nos. 3/4, 1999, focus on strategies taken by individual libraries faced with difficult planning challenges, as well as on information technology planning from the user's perspective.

Green, Kenneth C. *Campus Computing 1996.* Encino, Calif.: Campus Computing, 1996.
"Begun in 1990, the Campus Computing Project focuses on the use of information technology in higher education. The project's national studies draw on qualitative and quantitative data to help inform faculty, campus administrators, and others interested in the use of information technology in American colleges and universities. The annual Campus Computing Survey is the largest continuing study of the role of information technology in U.S. higher education. Each year more than 600 two- and four-year public and private colleges and universities participate in this survey, which focuses on campus planning and policy affecting the role of information technology in teaching, learning, and scholarship." (For additional information, see *www.campuscomputing.net*, accessed 10 June 1999.)

Hulser, Richard P. "Integrating Technology into Strategic Planning." *Information Outlook* 2, no. 2 (1998): 24–27.
This article directly addresses technology planning within a strategic planning framework within the context of the corporate library setting. The author discusses the establishment of a strategic planning team and the importance of aligning the plan with the organization's mission.

Lynch, Clifford A. "The Technological Framework for Library Planning in the Next Decade." *New Directions for Higher Education* 90 (Summer 1995): 93–105.
This article discusses trends that the author believes will define the future technological framework for academic research libraries. "The library of the next decade will answer the demands of its changing community rather than implement new technology to facilitate traditional operations."

Planning for Results: A Public Library Transformation Process. Chicago: Public Library Association, 1998.
This book "provides a unique, results-driven program that empowers librarians to meet community needs and to develop strategies to anticipate future demands." It includes an introductory Guidebook that explains each step in the planning process, and a How-To Manual that contains detailed instructions on how to perform each step in the process.

1

What Is a Technology Plan?

A technology plan identifies what systems and services will fulfill your library's mission and best meet user needs. It also provides a framework for the evaluation of services and products. The foundation of any technology plan is your library's long-range or strategic plan, which outlines the library's service mission, goals, and objectives. The technology plan may be integrated within the long-range plan itself, included as an addendum, or be a separate but related document.

A technology plan should be "strategic" in nature, whether or not you use that term to describe the plan. Strategic means that you are focusing on what you intend to accomplish within a multiyear time frame and how you expect to accomplish your objectives. The "how," in turn, is dependent on a number of key variables, such as underlying assumptions guiding the library's service program, strengths and weaknesses in the library's operating environment, and who is and who is not participating in the planning process.

For some, the purpose of a technology plan is to establish what kinds of hardware, software, telecommunications, and technical support the library will need three, five, or more years hence. While such projections may be part of a technology plan, they are not the primary purpose for writing one. The technology landscape is continuously changing and transforming. It is usually impossible to know with any precision what you will need six months or a year down the road, much less several years into the future. Moreover, a shopping list unrelated to institutional purpose is just that—a shopping list. It is not a planning tool and it does not serve to further library goals and objectives.

WHAT IS THE PURPOSE OF A TECHNOLOGY PLAN?

A technology plan has several purposes, all of which interrelate in some fashion:

1. *Technology plans are required for funding.* At a very basic level, funding authorities may require technology plans as a precondition for receiving money. The most obvious examples are the Federal Communications Commission's Universal Service program, and the Library Services and Technology Act, both of which provide financial assistance to public and school libraries and consortia. Applicants must describe their strategies for using information technologies and demonstrate how they plan to integrate technology into their curricula or service plans.

2. *Technology must be aligned with institutional priorities.* Everyone agrees that technology is just a tool. But computer and networking technologies are expensive tools. Governing bodies and parent institutions will want to know that expenditures for technologies are cost-effective and that they will efficiently carry forward the mission of the library and, in turn, the larger organization—the town, campus, corporation, or school district. A carefully designed plan will relate technology goals to broader, institutional goals.

3. *Libraries must establish alliances to further their technology goals.* For the library to accomplish its purposes, it must secure support from the "outside." Government officials, faculty, superintendents, and CFOs must "buy into" what the library wants to do. Technology planning enables the library to involve such individuals in a process through which they can establish "ownership" in the library's goals, thereby facilitating and ensuring success for the library's efforts.

4. *Technology plans are crucial to lobbying efforts.* As noted, modern technology is an expensive proposition. As a rule, libraries cannot simply shift monies around in existing budgets, which are often in decline anyway, to fund electronic technol-

ogy; therefore, the library's leadership must mount a lobbying campaign to secure special allocations or budgetary supplements. A well-formulated, thoughtful plan is crucial here; the library simply will not be taken seriously without such a document.

5. *Planning demonstrates proactiveness.* One of the chief criticisms often leveled against requests for technology funding is that they are just an attempt to acquire the latest gadget or "toy." Having a plan in place is never a guarantee that such a response will not occur, but it does lessen the likelihood. Again, it is a matter of relating technology needs to established and articulated principles of service. Think of it as the equivalent of writing and updating a collection development statement; having one does not preclude battles over censorship, but it does give you an important weapon—one that demonstrates forethought and planning—when the onslaught begins.

6. *Writing and revising a technology plan keeps everyone up-to-date.* While technology plans must be more than shopping lists, they must reflect what actually exists "out there" and must incorporate a high level of knowledge and understanding of technology's potential. Along with addressing the needs of the library, planning compels the participants to learn about specific technologies, trends, and developments in computing, networking, and the use of electronic applications to improve service.

THE IMPORTANCE OF THE PROCESS

All of the above suggests that perhaps as important as the technology plan is, the process of planning is at least of equal importance. Martin Ringle and Daniel Updegrove (1998) quote Dwight D. Eisenhower's comment—"In preparing for battle, I have always found that plans are useless, but planning is indispensable." While a book such as this clearly does not perceive plans as useless, the crucial role played by the actual planning is undeniable. Whether it is learning about technology, securing buy-in, or establishing the library's credibility, what is achieved during the process is as consequential as the output of that process.

Finally, we are all aware of how difficult change is for many people. The rapid, sometimes dizzying, pace of technological change has probably raised the tolerance level for some, while lowering it for others. In our book *Planning for Automation*, we referred to planning as a means of demystifying what at first appears overwhelming. Kathleen Imhoff (1996) has a section in her book called "Taking the Fear Out of Change." This is perhaps one of the most important aspects of technology planning: introducing change, then producing a framework and a guide—the technology plan—for managing it in the years ahead.

SOURCES

Cohn, John M., Ann L. Kelsey, and Keith Michael Fiels. *Planning for Automation: A How-To-Do-It Manual for Librarians.* 2nd ed. New York: Neal-Schuman, 1997.
This "guide to the essential components of automation planning" argues that a step-by-step approach will allow librarians to overcome the apprehension of what may appear as the daunting nature of technology planning and implementation.

Feinman, Valerie Jackson. "Five Steps toward Planning Today for Tomorrow's Needs." *Computers in Libraries* 19, no. 1 (1999): 18–21.
This article discusses the role of the library in the strategic planning for technologies process in colleges and universities. It includes an analysis of why planning is important and describes a five-step planning process.

Imhoff, Kathleen R. T. *Making the Most of New Technology: A How-To-Do-It Manual for Librarians.* New York: Neal-Schuman, 1996.
This book "provides guidelines for preparing a technology plan, coping tools, and an in-depth look at factors that will affect dealing with change and technological planning."

Jones, A. James. "Strategic Planning for Technology and Library Media Specialists." *School Library Media Quarterly* 24, no. 2 (1996): 119–21.
This article presents an overview of the technology planning process in a middle school setting, emphasizing the importance of

developing a technology plan that fits into an organization's overall goals and objectives.

Ringle, Martin & Daniel Updegrove. "Is Strategic Planning for Technology an Oxymoron?" EDUCAUSE Information Resources Library. *www.educause.edu/ir/library/html/cem9814.html* (Accessed 10 June 1999)
This paper, originally published in *Cause/Effect*, volume 21, number 1, 1998, presents an overview of technology planning in an academic environment. It discusses the purposes of technology planning, suggests why strategic technology planning sometimes fails, and offers suggestions for a successful outcome.

State of Wisconsin. Wisconsin Department of Public Instruction. Public Library Development. *Library Technology Planning.* 1998, March 20—last update. *www.dpi.state.wi.us/dlcl/pld/planout.html* (Accessed 10 June 1999)
This site provides an excellent outline of technology planning, including five factors deemed critical to effective library technology planning and implementation. It includes links to various Web-based resources useful in helping to develop technology plans.

Tebbetts, Diane R. "Building the Digital Library Infrastructure: A Primer." In *Information Technology Planning*, edited by Lori A. Goetsch. New York: Haworth Press, 1999, 5–23.
This article reviews the "elements necessary to support the interactive and dynamic nature of the digital library," including database development, OPACs, networking, hardware and wiring, licensing, authentication, and security. A concluding section argues the case for making careful technology planning a part of the process.

Walster, Diane. "Planning For Technology." *Journal of Library Administration* 22, no. 1 (1995) 39–50.
This article examines the positive and negative aspects of applying strategic and tactical planning methodologies to the integration and implementation of technology in libraries.

2

The Basic Components of a Technology Plan

As the plans included on the CD demonstrate, no two components are exactly alike. They are all organized and formatted differently and all respond to varying institutional, environmental, and library-specific imperatives.

While plans will vary from library to library, every successful technology plan contains the following basic components in some form:

- an executive summary
- background information
- the current state of technology
- the library's technology plan and budget
- an evaluation plan.

THE EXECUTIVE SUMMARY

Every plan should include an executive summary that offers a synopsis of the plan's major recommendations and conclusions.

A one-page executive summary is useful when a plan is more than a dozen pages in length. Even for shorter plans, an executive summary of one or two paragraphs is often included at the beginning of a plan as an introduction. The purpose of the executive summary is to highlight major recommendations, goals, or initiatives within the plan. A one-page executive summary can also be used independently of the plan as a fact sheet that can be included in information packets or used with funding authorities.

Examples of different but equally effective executive summaries include the University of California—Berkeley Media Resources Center, Multimedia Server Project; University of Florida Health Science Center Libraries, in narrative form; and the Kansas City, Missouri, and Hingham, Massachusetts, Public Libraries, which are essentially outlines of major goals and objectives.

BACKGROUND INFORMATION

This section of the plan provides information on the library, the community or constituency it serves, its organizational context, other plans, the external environment, and how the plan was developed.

An Overview of the Library, Its Mission, and the Community or User Group It Serves

Basic information about the library and its community should be included in the plan. This can be as brief as a paragraph or much longer if needed in order to establish the setting within which the library operates. A library serving a community with large numbers of home computer users, for example, is likely to develop a very different plan than a library serving a community with few home computer users. A library serving corporate clientele will approach technology differently than one serving students.

Likewise, the library's mission will affect the library's approach to technology. Examples from two equally excellent public library missions show how approaches and priorities can vary:

> The Rochester Hills Public Library provides up-to-date materials and information to people of all ages for their recreation, education, and lifelong learning. The library emphasizes efficient, convenient access and courteous, professional service in welcoming surroundings.

> The Trustees have charged us with the responsibility to act as a focal institution and system for publicly supported access by individuals to information, knowledge, and reading in Mont-

clair. . . . In a multi-cultural environment, the Library strives to act as a facilitator, organizer, and provider of information about the community and local government.

An example of a very different vision more typical of a special library:

> The mission of the U.S. Army Corps of Engineers Library Program is to retrieve and disseminate information, as well as to provide access to information resources and services with a firm commitment to delivering the right information, at the right price, in the right format, to the right people, at the right time.

The following is an example from a group of research libraries:

> The mission of the New York State Comprehensive Research Libraries is to work collaboratively to bring together, from all corners of the State, digitized materials that will: promote the economic and efficient delivery of research resources to the people of New York State; ensure public access to the rich resources in New York State; and, contribute to the national effort to develop digital libraries.

Sometimes, the library's overall vision statement may be cited here, if the library has one and it provides insight into how technology will be used in the delivery of services. This may be separate from a vision of how technology will be used by the library. Such a vision statement will appear as part of the technology plan section along with goals and objectives.

An Overview of the Process Used to Develop the Plan

This section provides a brief overview of how the plan was developed, who participated in the development of the plan, and an overview of key points in the planning process and may contain the names of people and organizations that participated in the development of the plan. If the planning committee is particularly large, a list of planning committee members or other planners may be attached as an addendum to the plan.

A particularly good example of a concise step-by-step description is included in the County College of Morris Technology Plan.

The Context of the Plan

Material describing organizational values or general assumptions may often be included to provide additional information on the context that shaped the plan and will guide its implementation.

This section should provide information on how the plan relates to or developed from previous documents or plans, or how the library's technology activities or goals relate to any plan developed by a parent institution. Often, the technology plan will be developed to complement a library's or organization's long-range plan. Information on this broader plan and its relationship to the technology plan will help place the activities described in the plan in perspective regarding the library or organization's service, research, educational, or business goals.

Many college and university plans include extensive discussions of the research environment or of trends in education and scholarship that affect the planning or institutional environment. Sometimes, a classic strategic analysis of organizational strengths, weaknesses, opportunities, and threats (SWOTs) will be included in this section; some historical perspectives are also included. The University of Wisconsin/Oshkosh plan is a good example of such an approach.

THE CURRENT STATE OF TECHNOLOGY

Every plan should describe the existing technology the library uses to support its service program. A description of current technology within the library and/or organization provides information on the foundation upon which future technology efforts will be built. Such a description or inventory is also a required component of any plan that is prepared to qualify the library for E-rate funding.

The inventory, sometimes supplemented with graphics or charts, will provide a detailed overview of the technological environment of the library, i.e., the library's current equipment, telecommunications services, software, and electronic resources. A subsequent chapter will review how such an inventory may be assembled.

The form and specificity of an inventory may vary quite a bit.

- In many plans, the entire inventory can be presented as a single page. A good example is the Batesville, Indiana, plan.
- The Burlington County, New Jersey, plan is a particularly clear presentation consisting of 1) a narrative describing technology-based services provided by the system, and 2) an equipment inventory consisting of a single page for each branch library (Figure 2–1).

While most technology inventories in the past have included information on hardware, integrated systems, and software applications, a library preparing an application for the E-rate program will also need information on a number of additional existing or projected technologies and services for which discounts may be requested. These specific services are:

A. Telecommunications services
   Telecommunications lines (voice and data)
       Voice/fax telephone
       Wireless service telephone (cellular phones, pagers, etc.)
       Computer workstations with modems (dial-access)
       Leased data circuits (i.e., OCLC, ISP—Internet service providers)
   Special telecommunications equipment (telecommunications devices for the deaf—TDD)
   Distance learning
       High bandwidth video conferencing links
       Video retrieval service providers
       Satellite service providers for distance learning

B. Internal Connections
   Equipment
       Hubs
       Routers
       Data wiring
       Network servers
   Other
       Network software
       Maintenance contracts

Figure 2–1 Burlington County Library System Equipment Inventory

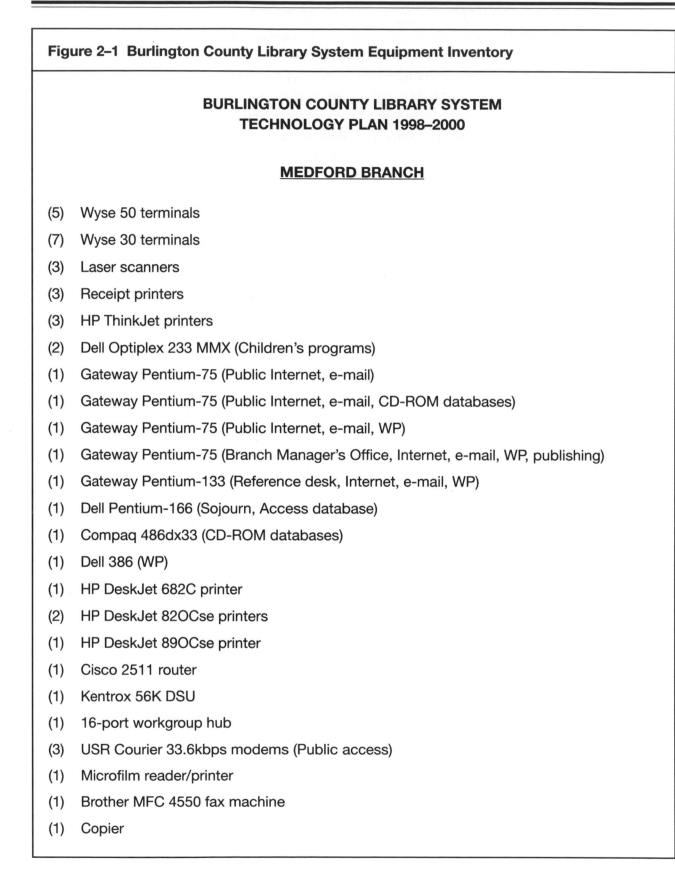

BURLINGTON COUNTY LIBRARY SYSTEM
TECHNOLOGY PLAN 1998–2000

MEDFORD BRANCH

(5)   Wyse 50 terminals

(7)   Wyse 30 terminals

(3)   Laser scanners

(3)   Receipt printers

(3)   HP ThinkJet printers

(2)   Dell Optiplex 233 MMX (Children's programs)

(1)   Gateway Pentium-75 (Public Internet, e-mail)

(1)   Gateway Pentium-75 (Public Internet, e-mail, CD-ROM databases)

(1)   Gateway Pentium-75 (Public Internet, e-mail, WP)

(1)   Gateway Pentium-75 (Branch Manager's Office, Internet, e-mail, WP, publishing)

(1)   Gateway Pentium-133 (Reference desk, Internet, e-mail, WP)

(1)   Dell Pentium-166 (Sojourn, Access database)

(1)   Compaq 486dx33 (CD-ROM databases)

(1)   Dell 386 (WP)

(1)   HP DeskJet 682C printer

(2)   HP DeskJet 82OCse printers

(1)   HP DeskJet 89OCse printer

(1)   Cisco 2511 router

(1)   Kentrox 56K DSU

(1)   16-port workgroup hub

(3)   USR Courier 33.6kbps modems (Public access)

(1)   Microfilm reader/printer

(1)   Brother MFC 4550 fax machine

(1)   Copier

C. Internet Access
   Internet Providers
      Dial-up connections (baud rate)
      Direct connections (T1, 56kbs, ISDN lines)
   E-mail accounts

THE LIBRARY'S TECHNOLOGY PLAN AND BUDGET

The Library's Technology Vision and Strategy

Stand-alone plans should begin with a technology vision statement and/or strategy. Plans prepared as part of the Universal Service program must include such a statement. The narrative section will describe how the library proposes to use technology. The vision statement should be consistent with any vision statement in the library's overall plan, providing a broad strategy for the use of technology in providing library services and describing how technology assists staff in carrying out the library's mission.

A vision statement describes what the library will "look like" if the plan is implemented. Generally, it is no more than three or four sentences. Examples of vision statements are:

Often the most effective way, and in some cases the only way, to access important resources is through audiovisual and digital technology. Therefore, it is the intention of the [Lake County Public] Library to implement the use of a wide variety of technological tools and resources that meet the needs of staff and patrons.

The Monroe Public Library, in fulfilling its role as the community media and information center, provides timely, accurate, and useful materials and services to satisfy the personal, educational, and professional needs of the community. Special emphasis is placed on providing current, high-demand, high-interest materials in a variety of formats to persons of all ages and on stimulating young children's interests and appreciation for reading and learning. Continuing efforts are made to respond to changing needs of the community and to evolving technological means of providing resources and services. The Library also serves as a resource for continuing education and community information for the Monroe community.

In the year 2000, the Kitsap Regional Library is the dynamic center of information access for the people of Kitsap County. The library is the first source that people consider for the answers to the questions that affect their everyday lives; they view it as an extension of their personal knowledge and memory. The library is a place where individuals, families, and organizations go to explore the world of knowledge and the record of culture.

A narrative outlining the library's technology strategy (a component of any Universal Service discount plan) expands on this vision and describes the major thrust of any existing or planned technology-related activities.

Goals and Objectives for the Improvement of Library Service

"Goals" are broad statements of intended outcome. In general, a plan will be organized under a half-dozen or so general goals. The best goals are user-oriented, in that they focus on the desired impact of the library on users or the community at large.
   Examples of goals include:

- Improve community access to information both within and from outside the library
- Improve the quality and efficiency of library services
- Regularly evaluate existing and emerging technology to assure the best possible public service
- Develop and implement electronic resources to provide information to people of all ages
- Cooperate with other libraries, governmental entities, and community organizations to improve the quality and efficiency of electronic resources
- Contribute to building and maintaining the world's knowledge base
- Develop instructional programs to support the University mission
- Provide an organizational structure for the digital library.

While goals are necessarily vague, they are a critical link between the mission of the library, the users the library serves, and the objectives and activities that support the attainment of each goal.

Goals may be grouped by major library functions or roles. A number of recently developed plans—Rochester Hills is a good example—organize goals by the following broad functions that, as in Rochester Hills' case, often echo functions in the library's long-range plan:

- Public services
- Staff services
- Collection development
- Facilities and equipment
- Community relations
- Interagency cooperation.

Such a broad functions-based approach is also consistent with the approach recommended in subsequent chapters on the planning process.

"Objectives" are narrower statements of intended shorter-term accomplishment organized under a goal. Objectives are more specific statements that outline how or how much of the goal will be fulfilled. Generally, objectives are as concrete and specific as possible.

Examples of objectives include:

- Implement client/server distributed processing throughout the system
- Expand the library's Web site by continually adding links to appropriate resources
- Create a digital library
- Create finding aids to assist in the location of digital materials located in the making of New York site
- Provide library users a common GUI (Graphical User Interface) to electronic resources.

We should note that the terms "goal" and "objective" are sometimes used interchangeably. (For instance, similar statements appear as goals in one plan and as objectives in another.) Sometimes, goals are amplified by subgoals. Whatever terms are used, more specific and particular statements will support broader and more general statements.

In developing your written plan, it is critical that your goals and objectives are as user-oriented as possible. What you want to do is less important than what it will do for your users. Luckily, your needs assessment work, described below, will help you to cast your plan with the user perspective in mind.

Technology Needs and Action Plan

"Activities" are specific steps or tasks undertaken to achieve an objective. Depending on what works best, they may be arranged in chronological order under your objectives or grouped by year. Examples of activities are:

- Work with the City of Rochester to develop a city home page by September 1997
- Make special collections' photographs available in digital format by December 1999
- Buy three network interface cards for branch PCs
- Replace all eight Wyse 50 dumb terminals with Pentium-based workstations
- Develop written policy for use of Internet and e-mail
- Continue to work with any task from year one that did not get completed due to time or money constraints.

Some plans will present groups of related activities as a series of "initiatives." In *Planning for Automation*, we stressed the need to provide for staff training as part of the overall plan. Under the requirements for the E-rate program, "Staff Training" is a required component. Some part of your plan should address these concerns, whether they are included as a separate goal or a separate objective, with appropriate activities to support it (and to include in your budget.)

Time and money are the distinguishing differences among goals and objectives and activities. Activities represent a specific amount of staff time and/or require a specific amount of money. This is where your budget begins.

The Costs of Needed Technology (A Proposed Budget)

This section of your plan will gather together all the equipment and services that will require purchase, as distinct from staff time and effort represented by your proposed activities. In most plans, this information is presented either as a budget request for the coming year or for a series of years on a year-by-year basis.

The phrase "technology needs" is used by the Universal Services' School and Libraries Division to refer to equipment and services that the library wishes to purchase. This is one instance in which a "laundry list" is perfectly acceptable, as long as it relates to your mission and technology strategy. Most libraries present this listing of needs with accompanying cost figures.

In a great number of instances, budgets are prepared and distributed as separate documents, and, as a result, are not included on the CD.

Some examples of approaches to presenting a budget include the one-page estimated budget of the Batesville Memorial Public Library (Figure 2–2), and the equally straightforward, if more lengthy, budgets of the Burlington County and Rochester Hills Public Libraries.

Figure 2–2 Batesville Memorial Public Library One-Page Estimated Budget

Batesville Memorial Public Library
Technology Plan for 1999–2001

Estimated Budget

Computer package for disabled users .... (grant)

TI Internet connection .... (grant)

Computer, software and locking cabinet for business use in Mary
    Stewart Center for Entrepreneurship $3,800.00

Additional CD-ROM titles 2,000.00

Computer with genealogy software, with scanner....................................... 3,400.00

Children's Reference Computer with software 3,000.00

Videoconferencing equipment 30,000.00

CD-ROM tower 4,000.00

Networking and installation costs 10,000.00

Programming costs for "technology literacy" sessions 500.00

Staff training costs 2,000.00

Technology maintenance and replacement costs....................................... 5,000.00

EVALUATION

The two basic components of an evaluation are generally measures of success and an evaluation process.

Generally, the evaluation ties specific measures to the achievement of an objective. (A simple example of this is the number of times a new service or technology is used.) Data collection and analysis are used to compare your actual results to your proposed target and to make corrections during the implementation process.

The plan should also describe a methodology and timetable for keeping the plan current. An evaluation process will provide for regular examination of the progress in achieving the plan and its goals, and ultimately for evaluating the effectiveness of the plan itself. This is particularly useful when the library begins to develop a new plan, by providing a sense of what about the plan was useful and what needs to be changed.

Many evaluation plans are quite simple, as this example illustrates:

> The library will conduct random patron surveys to measure their satisfaction with new services. The surveys will be conducted for a two-week period and then will be evaluated by the Director and the Board of Trustees.
>
> As the new services are implemented, the staff will keep careful records of the number of patrons using each service. The records will help the library when new services are being contemplated in the future.
>
> The library will keep careful records of the use of each computer used for Internet access. These figures will help to determine if the library will need additional computers and in which area of the library the computers are used.

A later chapter in this book discusses further the issue of evaluating the library's technology plan.

WHAT SHOULD I INCLUDE IN MY PLAN?

It is important that the basic elements described above be part of any plan. How and in what manner they are presented will depend on the library's intended audience and what purpose the library hopes to accomplish. In particular, libraries that must meet submission requirements imposed by an external funding agency should compare this outline to the agency's published guidelines and adjust its format accordingly.

Plans that are developed as part of the E-rate program must contain certain required components. These are outlined in Figure 2–3. With a little planning and some forethought, these components can easily be addressed as you develop your plan, as discussed in this chapter. Sometimes, a specific label is all that is required to identify those parts of your plan that meet E-rate requirements.

The library's technology plan must be a comprehensive document that can be broken out into modular components for special needs and funding opportunities. The library must realize that the same document that is used to secure funding might also serve as a public relations piece for informing and generating public, corporate, faculty, and/or administrative support. Making revisions and adjustments of style and emphasis in a document that is complete from the start is much easier than having to assemble new materials in order to address different audiences and purposes.

Figure 2–3 Universal Service Technology Plan Criteria

To qualify as an approved Technology Plan for a Universal Service discount, the plan must meet the following five criteria that are core elements of successful school and library technology initiatives:

(1) the plan must establish clear goals and a realistic strategy for using telecommunications and information technology to improve education or library services;

(2) the plan must have a professional development strategy to ensure that staff know how to use these new technologies to improve education or library services;

(3) the plan must include an assessment of the telecommunication services, hardware, software, and other services that will be needed to improve education or library services;

(4) the plan must provide for a sufficient budget to acquire and maintain the hardware, software, professional development, and other services that will be needed to implement the strategy; and

(5) the plan must include an evaluation process that enables the school or library to monitor progress toward the specified goals and make mid-course corrections in response to new developments and opportunities as they arise.

Successful plans align these five criteria with the overall education or library service improvement objectives of states, districts, and local schools or libraries. It is critical that technology planning not be viewed or treated as a separate exercise dealing primarily with hardware and telecommunications infrastructure. There must be strong connections between the proposed physical infrastructure of the information technology and the plan for professional development, curriculum reform, and library service improvements.

Source: "SLC Technology Plan Policies and Procedures" (1/5/98)

SOURCES

Cohn, John M., Ann L. Kelsey, and Keith Michael Fiels. *Planning for Automation: A How-To-Do-It for Librarians*. 2nd ed. New York: Neal-Schuman. 1997.
Chapters 3 and 4 discuss goals and objectives in the context of strategic planning for technology.

Guidebook for Developing an Effective Instructional Technology Plan. Mississippi State University, National Center for Technology Planning, 1996.
This 45-page guide provides a simple technology planning model for planners. It has a section on the process of planning and a section on the product of planning—your technology planning document. A section on critical issues provides a concise checklist of potential areas that academic and school library planners may wish to address.

Jacob, M.E.L. *Strategic Planning: A How-To-Do-It Manual for Librarians*. New York: Neal-Schuman, 1990.
A practical hands-on manual with checklists, workforms, and samples, this book includes a chapter on Strategic Focus, in which goals, objectives, and action plans are discussed.

Universal Service Administrative Company (USAC). Schools and Libraries Division. *SLC Technology Plan Policies and Procedures (1/5/98)*. 1997. April 15, 1999—last update.
www.sl.universalservice.org/Reference/Tech_Plan_docs/explain_tech.asp (Accessed 11 June 1999.)
This site provides explanations of the USAC's technology plan policies and procedures. Plan criteria are set forth, along with information concerning the length and scope of the plan, the technology plan approval process, audits, and contact information.

Walster, Diane. "Planning for Technology." *Journal of Library Administration* 22, no. 1, (1995): 39–50.
A discussion of the techniques of *strategic* planning, which provides a focus for the future, and *tactical* planning, which emphasizes the more routine needs of the present. The article provides a good checklist of considerations to help strategic planners develop more "implementable" plans and tactical planners to focus on organizational context and goals.

3

Defining Your Plan: Some Basic Decisions

Much of the variety in the scope and appearance of individual plans is a direct result of a number of basic decisions that you will need to make early in the process. Your decisions will, to a large extent, determine the "look" of your final plan.

DECISION 1: WHO IS YOUR INTENDED AUDIENCE?

Deciding who the audience is for the plan is probably the most important decision. Is the plan intended for the general public? Is it intended for your parent organization's technical staff or administrative staff? Is it intended for your funding body as a method of gaining support for a budget request?

The answer to these questions will affect your style, vocabulary, and the amount and nature of information you will want to include in your plan.

DECISION 2: WHAT IS YOUR PLANNING "HORIZON"?

A survey of library plans conducted a number of years ago revealed that library plans varied considerably in scope. One library even reported a planning horizon of one hundred years!

The most basic unit of planning is generally a year, based on the library or organization's budget cycle. Most public library long-range plans are five-year plans. Sometimes, when a plan is in fact a plan for a specific project, the time period is determined by the project implementation timetable and may be less than a year or several years. While the vast majority of libraries that developed plans for the federal E-rate discount initially developed one-year plans, the Schools and Libraries Corporation now recommends three-year plans. Given the realities of the annual budget cycle, multiyear plans will generally be presented as annual increments for budgeting purposes.

If your library is part of a parent organization, your planning horizon will be determined for you. Otherwise, a three-year plan will probably be your best choice.

DECISION 3: STRATEGIC PLAN OR ACTION PLAN?

An "action plan" is a straightforward step-by-step plan for accomplishing your objectives, based on the assumption that your resources are known and under your control. If you are developing a multiyear plan and you cannot absolutely predict the rate at which financial resources will become available to implement your action plan, or your actual implementation strategy is not absolutely clear due to circumstances outside your control, such as when consortial arrangements need to be articulated, a "strategic plan" may be more suitable. In general, a strategic plan focuses on your desired outcomes in the form of a "vision" of ideal service for your users rather than the specific methods for attaining that vision.

Often, plans will contain certain strategic components such as an environmental analysis or vision statement or organizational values, and also include an action plan for the initial year.

DECISION 4: HOW EXTENSIVE WILL THE NEEDS ASSESSMENT BE?

Identifying user needs is usually the most difficult and labor-intensive part of any planning process. Approaches to needs assessment include surveys, analysis of usage data, analysis of data on unfilled requests, user suggestions, one-on-one interviews, focus groups, and structured group process—and sometimes all of the above.

On the other hand, needs assessments can be as straightforward as those who are developing the plan simply writing down the things they would like to purchase if they had more money. Obviously, this is a lot easier, but not always the best approach if you need to sell your plan.

User involvement in developing the plan will help you to develop more user-oriented goals and will certainly help shape your decisions regarding your priorities.

DECISION 5: HOW DOES THIS PLAN RELATE TO THE PLANS OF OTHER ORGANIZATIONS?

For most public libraries, the development of a stand-alone technology plan will be your first choice, but a number of decisions will need to be made about how the technology plan will be related to your library's long-range plan.

- How extensively will you quote such things as your library's mission and any vision statement for the library?

- Will you relate your technology objectives and activities to your library's overall goals, or does your library have a technology goal under which your technology plan will be organized?

If your library is an academic, special, or school library, your technology plan will most likely be incorporated into a technology plan for your parent organization. Your plan may be developed as part of an organizational effort, or you may be updating the library portion of an organizational plan. Optimally, you will have developed a short technology plan for the library that you can bring to your parent organization. In general, you should assume that the more developed your plan is, the more likely you are to see it included in the organizational plan.

If you are a member of a consortium, a large part of your technology plan may be determined as part of the consortium plan. You will need to decide how extensively you will quote this plan and what information from it you will need to include in your own technology plan.

While the preponderance of planning activity in academic, school, and special libraries will occur at the institutional level, it is advisable that any academic, school, or special library that can mount a needs assessment and develop its own library plan do so. With such a plan, the library will ultimately be more successful in securing the inclusion of library-related goals, objectives, activities, and budget initiatives in the final institutional plan. Such planning must be undertaken with the support of and with a clear commitment to the support of annual institutional goals.

SOURCES

Balas, Janet L. "Online Help For Library Strategic Planners." *Computers in Libraries* 19, no. 1 (1999): 40–42.
While the focus is on strategic planning, this article also includes references to technology plans prepared by diverse organizations, including academic library consortia and association divisions.

Harley, Bruce. "Planning For Sustainable Automation." *Information Technology and Libraries* 14, no. 3 (1995): 176–79.
This thoughtful and interesting article approaches technology planning from the point of view of sustainability. The author suggests that the possibility of organizational instability during the implementation of technology can be alleviated by utilizing the elements of sustainable development—for example, an environmental perspective and ecological values—in the technology planning process.

Hopwood, Susan H. "Long-Range Planning and Funding For Innovation." *Computers in Libraries* 19, no. 1 (1999): 22–27.
This article describes in detail the strategic and technology planning processes engaged in by the Marquette University libraries. URLs are provided for viewing the documents on the Web. The interrelationships between strategic and technology plans are clearly defined and illustrated in the text.

4

Developing Your Plan: Gathering Data and Identifying Needs

INTRODUCTION

Over the years, libraries and organizations generally have become more accepting of the need for systematic planning as a way of ensuring success. Whether as cause or effect, the literature contains many works offering methodologies that are designed to assist planners with the intricacies of long-range and strategic planning. The text authored by John M. Bryson, *Strategic Planning for Public and Nonprofit Organizations* (1995) and the accompanying workbook by Bryson and Farnum K. Alston, *Creating and Implementing Your Strategic Plan* (1996), for example, are considered standards in the field. The 1984 book (now out of print) by Donald E. Riggs, *Strategic Planning for Library Managers*, is one of the most clearly written and concise volumes prepared specifically for librarians on the strategic planning process.

Similarly, you can now find an array of Internet-based guides and a few published works on the ins-and-outs of producing strategic technology plans. One of the most recent and significant of the latter is Diane Mayo and Sandra Nelson's *Wired for the Future* (1999), which was produced for the Public Library Association and published by the American Library Association. This work is aimed at taking the reader through a process that focuses on assessing technology-based products and the technical infrastructure, encompassing software, hardware, networks, and telecommunications, that is required "to deliver those products to your customers." Detailing 16 tasks, and replete with 20 work forms and activity planners, the book offers a comprehensive and elaborate approach to developing a technology plan.

Decision makers must decide how intricate and complex they require or intend the planning process to be. This book assumes the need for an expeditious process that results in a plan that addresses all the key issues in implementing or updating technology in the library. Accordingly, this chapter and Chapter 5 outline a series of relatively simple steps for developing or updating a technology plan.

INITIAL STEPS IN DEVELOPING THE PLAN

There are three important initial steps that must be taken in developing a technology plan. They are:

1. Identifying stakeholder participants in the planning process;
2. Identifying the library's existing programs and services and the technologies that support them; and,
3. Gathering data and identifying present and future needs.

These steps are preparatory in nature but will remain part of the planning process throughout. Together, they will provide both raw material for decision making and a framework for writing the actual plan.

Identifying Stakeholder Participants

Stakeholders are those persons who, very simply, have a stake in what your library does or does not do. Stakeholders include:

1. Clients, patrons, members, the public—whatever term or terms you use to describe the people you are in business to serve;
2. Employees, staff, volunteers—those individuals who provide your library's services;
3. Boards, "friends" groups, agencies—funding and/or govern-

ing and support organizations as well as related institutions that have an interest in the work of your library.

As you begin your planning process, you will need to identify who your stakeholders are and how you hope to involve them in the process. Not everyone needs or will want to be involved to the same degree. For example, the library's staff or the members of a consortium may participate fully in all parts of the process, while a dean, supervisor, or board member may want only to be "kept up to speed" about what is going on. Some will be involved at certain points but not at other times.

It is important that you are clear on what you hope to accomplish by involving your stakeholders. From some people, you will get information, ideas, and suggestions that will move your process forward in measurable or creative ways. Others may contribute less, but they have a need to be consulted and will feel left out if they are not. The most impressive technology plan may falter if significant numbers/categories of stakeholders feel that the plan was developed without their involvement. Apart from perhaps failing to address certain important concerns, you may risk compromising the plan's success simply because stakeholders question the process used to create it.

Identifying Existing Services and Technologies

In *Planning for Automation*, the authors identified four basic functions of libraries in an electronic age:

1. Providing access to the content of local resources (e.g., books, periodicals, media, electronic resources) that are part of the library's collection;
2. Offering gateway access to remote resources (e.g., books, periodicals, media, electronic resources), including the ability to obtain copies in print and electronic formats;
3. Facilitating offsite electronic access to local and remote resources from users' homes, offices, and schools; and,
4. Providing access to human assistance and training in locating information.

Each of these functions is described in more detail in Figure 4–1.

Figure 4–1 Library Functions in an Electronic Age

Function	Description
Access to the content of local resources that are part of the library's collection—e.g., books, periodicals, media, electronic resources.	Includes the shelving and display of hardcopy and other library materials as well as access (via library workstations) to an automated catalog containing bibliographic records, locally created electronic resources, and files created by external providers and stored locally. All files are searchable by author, title, subject, and other indexed descriptors.
Access via gateway to remote resources, e.g., books, periodicals, media, electronic resources, with the ability to obtain copies in print or electronic format.	Encompasses accessing from library workstations those resources not residing at the local library. Users can search for information by author, title, subject, and other descriptors, which lead them to bibliographic records, abstracts, the full text of documents, and other textual, graphic, and multimedia files. Materials are obtainable through online interlibrary loan request or via electronic transmission, with provision for copyright compliance and the secure transmission of billing information.
Electronic access to local and remote resources from offsite locations such as homes, offices, and schools.	Includes direct access to local library systems via telephone dial-up or through the Internet.
Access to assistance and training in locating information.	On-site trained librarians provide this function, serving as the human interface to all information services, either in person or remotely via electronic mail or video conferencing, and by the development of tutorials, often online.

Use these basic functional categories as a framework for identifying your library's programs and services and for describing existing technologies employed to support these services. A Basic Technology Assessment Worksheet, presented as Figure 4–2, can help you to organize your information on:

- Existing automated services
- Data files (e.g., bibliographic records, patron files)
- Computer and peripheral hardware
- Telecommunications and connectivity
- Application and operating system software.

While inventories can be organized by system, by physical location, or by function, the authors recommend the breakdown described above because it helps to ensure that all your "laundry lists" of equipment are organized in the most meaningful fashion according to what they provide to your users. This end-user orientation is particularly useful if you are trying to secure resources in a competitive environment.

It is a challenging process to develop a comprehensive, detailed inventory of existing technologies in the library; however, it is a necessary step in developing or updating your technology plan and in assessing the current and future needs of your users. Moreover, such an inventory is a required component in some grant applications, such as the one for the E-rate discount.

Figure 4–2 Basic Technology Assessment Worksheet

	What automated services are currently provided to support this program or service?	What data files currently exist to support this program or service?	What computer and peripheral hardware currently support this program or service?	What telecommunications/ connectivity currently exists to support this program or service?	What software currently supports this program or service?
Program or service					
Program or service					
Program or service					
Program or service					
Program or service					
Program or service					
Program or service					
Program or service					
Program or service					

Gathering Data and Identifying Needs

The next step is to gather information on what services stakeholders would like to have available from your library that your library is not currently providing. It is also useful for evaluating existing services and the technologies that support them.

This step usually involves one or more of the following methodologies:

- **Analyzing information on existing use**
  Existing use patterns can help to identify areas of need. Highly used services may need to be further expanded, little used services improved. Of particular benefit are any data you may gather regarding unfilled request or user complaints.

- **Distributing written user surveys**
  Planning groups are frequently tempted to undertake extensive surveys; however, the results of such surveys may be difficult to translate into specific needs. A series of short surveys will often produce much higher response rates and can be developed at specific points in the needs assessment or planning process to shed light on particular questions or issues.

- **Holding focus groups, interviews, or informal discussions with stakeholders**
  Interviews or informal discussions can be very useful in identifying problems in existing services and systems or in discovering what users and others (including staff) really need. A more formal process is to organize focus groups—small groups of people getting together to discuss specific topics. Focus groups are widely used to generate the kind of information that is difficult to obtain using written surveys, including perceptions and needs that people find difficult to articulate.

  Many libraries have found that a one-day process for bringing stakeholders and users together, identifying needs, and gathering information on priorities is an effective approach. Such a process is reasonably easy to manage and will save considerable time and money over many more sophisticated approaches.

- **Analyzing services provided by comparable or competitor libraries**
  Finally, consider examining the programs and services of other libraries serving comparable user populations, emphasizing those libraries that have achieved recognition for their outstanding efforts. What services do they offer that your library does not?

A Basic Needs Assessment Worksheet, which can be used to summarize the findings of your data gathering activities, is given in Figure 4–3. In this fashion, you can ascertain how your services are perceived by your stakeholders and perhaps determine, based upon the input you receive, how they should be prioritized.

The data that you have collected by means of the worksheets described in this chapter will assist you in preparing and writing your technology strategic plan. That is the subject of the next chapter.

Figure 4–3 Basic Needs Assessment Worksheet

	How is the program or service being provided currently?	What problems or limitations exist with the way this program or service is provided?	Ideally, how should this program or service be provided?	What is the priority for this program or service based upon user input?
Program or service				
Program or service				
Program or service				
Program or service				
Program or service				
Program or service				
Program or service				
Program or service				
Program or service				

SOURCES

Boss, Richard W. "Model Technology Plans for Libraries." *Library Technology Reports* 34, no. 1 (January/February, 1998), 114pp. This volume of *LTR* offers an Information Technology Overview and Trends section that discusses automated library systems, CD-ROM, online reference services, the Internet, networks, as well as other automated systems found in libraries. Model technology plans are presented for a single library, a library system, and a consortium. A model grant application is also included.

Bryson, John M. *Strategic Planning for Public and Nonprofit Organizations; A Guide to Strengthening and Sustaining Organizational Achievement.* Revised ed. San Francisco: Jossey-Bass, 1995. This book reviews the importance of strategic planning for organizations and communities, presents a model strategic planning process, offers guidance on applying the process, discusses the roles played by individuals and groups in the process, and includes examples of both successful and unsuccessful strategic planning practices.

Bryson, John M., and Farnum K. Alston. *Creating and Implementing Your Strategic Plan: A Workbook for Public and Nonprofit Organizations.* San Francisco: Jossey-Bass, 1996.
This work is intended to be used in tandem with the revised edition of *Strategic Planning for Public and Nonprofit Organizations* (Bryson, 1995). The book outlines and describes each of ten proposed steps to be employed in strategic planning and offers worksheets to facilitate the process.

Cohn, John M., Ann L. Kelsey, and Keith Michael Fiels. *Planning for Automation: A How-To-Do-It Manual for Librarians.* 2nd ed. New York: Neal-Schuman, 1997.
Part I covers the creation of a basic technology plan and includes a model one-day planning process.

Greenbaum, Thomas L. *The Handbook for Focus Group Research.* San Francisco: Jossey-Bass, 1993.
This book discusses the planning, conducting, and reporting of focus group activity. It provides an overview of the technique and many examples of its use.

Krueger, Richard A. *Focus Groups: A Practical Guide for Applied Research*. 2nd ed. Thousand Oaks, Calif.: Sage, 1994.
Particular attention is paid to the analysis and reporting of focus group results. The numerous examples will be especially useful to those who are just getting started.

Mayo, Diane, and Sandra Nelson, for the Public Library Association. *Wired for the Future: Developing Your Library Technology Plan*. Chicago: American Library Association, 1999.
The book's planning tasks are described in depth in five chapters:
- Preparing to Plan
- Identifying Technology Needs
- Discovering Options
- Selecting a Technology Infrastructure and Identifying Products and Services
- Developing and Managing the Implementation Process

"Tech Notes" offers descriptions of current technologies, from "Building Wire to Z39.50."

Riggs, Donald E. *Strategic Planning for Library Managers*. Phoenix: Oryx Press (out of print), 1984.
This book offers a helping hand to managers, so that they may better understand and assess where their libraries currently are, where they are going, and what the best ways are to get them to where they want to go. It is a succinct state-of-the-art document on strategic planning, including a descriptive narration of the interrelationships of the various components of a strategic plan and a "how to do it" prescriptive approach for effective implementation.

Sudman, Seymour, and Norman A. Bradburn. *Asking Questions: A Practical Guide to Questionnaire Design*. San Francisco: Jossey-Bass, 1986.
This book gives a detailed treatment of question design, with sections on the order and format of the questionnaire, the design of telephone and mail surveys, and a step-by-step questionnaire checklist.

5
Preparing and Writing Your Technology Plan

As a result of the activities described in the previous chapter, you have inventoried your existing technology and surveyed your library's stakeholders to assess their perceived service needs and priorities. In the present chapter, we focus on the actual preparation of the plan.

REFINING YOUR PRIORITIES

Remember that one of the most important factors in writing your technology plan is to ensure stakeholder participation in the plan's development. You have already solicited stakeholder input by conducting a needs assessment. You can now provide an opportunity for these and/or other stakeholders to articulate their perceptions, hopes, and concerns in a structured, facilitated setting designed to result in the generation of ideas that are then shaped into the elements of a plan.

Ideas can be generated through simple brainstorming exercises involving the recording of ideas on newsprint. The newsprint is then posted around the planning site for everyone to view. Following these exercises, participants can be asked to assign point values to the posted ideas. In this manner, you can establish the relative importance of these ideas to the stakeholders. Together with the results of your needs assessment, you have the material you need to develop your plan's goals, objectives, and action steps.

DEVELOPING GOALS, OBJECTIVES, AND ACTION STEPS

We made the point earlier that your library's mission or vision of service should drive its technology plan, not the other way around. To that vision of service should now be added elements discussed previously:

- *Goals*: Broad statements of desired or intended long-term accomplishment based upon the mission;
- *Objectives*: Narrower assertions of desired or intended shorter-term accomplishments designed to achieve a goal. Objectives outline how and how much of the goal will be fulfilled in as concrete and specific a way as possible;
- *Actions*: Measurable activities, often in a specific time frame, undertaken to achieve an objective.

How do you go about shaping these elements of the plan?

First, you must decide how far you wish to go with your stakeholders. A group experienced in the joys of "process" activity might be able to work together to transform your raw data into a plan. Alternatively, you can create a smaller team to construct the actual plan. That plan can then be circulated among the members of the larger group for comments, suggestions, and revisions.

Secondly, you will have to relate your proposed goal structure to the previously identified functions of your library. A Technology Planning Worksheet (Figure 5–1) offers a format that will enable you to align your proposed goals, objectives, and actions with these functions.

Finally, your plan should conform as much as possible in format, structure, and use of terminology to other planning documents within your organization. You must communicate consistency and a sense of "inter-relatedness" to your constituencies.

Figure 5–1 Technology Planning Worksheet

Statement of Purpose:

Function	Goal*	Objective*	Action*
Access to the content of local resources that are part of the library's collection, e.g., books, periodicals, media, electronic resources			
Access via gateway to remote resources, e.g., books, etc., with the ability to obtain copies in print or electronic format			
Electronic access to local and remote resources from offsite locations such as homes, offices, and schools			
Access to human assistance in locating information			

*Use a separate worksheet for each goal, objective, and act on statement, since each function is likely to generate multiple goals with multiple objectives and actions in turn.

DEVELOPING A BUDGET AND TIMETABLE FOR IMPLEMENTATION

With your goals, objectives and action items in place, it is time to consider the costs of your plan and developing a time frame for implementing it.

Cost Factors

Implementing or upgrading technology involves certain categories of expenditure. Not all of these may apply in each library's situation at any given point in time. The categories of expenditure are as follows:

1. *Planning and consulting*—Direct (out-of-pocket) and indirect (time is money!) costs of putting together your technology plan.
2. *Computer hardware and peripheral equipment*—Network servers, workstations, printers, and other machine peripherals, as well as site preparation for the equipment.
3. *Application and network software/licensing*—Integrated system applications, licenses, network operating system software.
4. *Cabling and telecommunications*—Wiring, network architecture, network interface cards, line charges (e.g., frame relay, ISDN, SMDS), hubs/routers/switches, Internet connectivity.
5. *Library database conversion*—Creating machine-readable bibliographic, user, and other records.
6. *Security*—Stand-alone equipment, operating system, database (firewalls), password authentication, proxy servers.
7. *External databases and systems*—Licensing, transaction and/or subscription costs associated with accessing full-text databases, images, audio and video.
8. *Training*—Vendor training, re-training, continuing education, professional development, and user education.
9. *Support*—Salaries of staff dedicated to technology and contracted services with outside vendors, e.g., third-party network integrators and developers.

For each of these, there are *initial costs* as well as *recurring costs* associated with subscription fees, database maintenance, equipment and software maintenance, salaries and contracted services, continuing education and training. Finally, there may be *upgrade* costs associated with accommodating new users, upgrading to improve performance, or adding functionality.

Figure 5–2 provides a Technology Cost Worksheet for use in planning the expenditures that must be incurred in carrying forward your plan.

The cost information you gather in your planning will allow you to present general budget estimates for each proposed component of your plan and to document your costs in detail as it is reviewed by your funding authorities.

Figure 5–2 Technology Cost Worksheet

Cost Factor	Service/activity			Service/activity		
	Initial costs	Recurring costs	Additional costs	Initial costs	Recurring costs	Additional costs
Planning and consulting						
Computer hardware and peripheral equipment						
Application and network software						
Cabling and telecommunications						
Library database conversion						
Security						
External databases and systems						
Training						
Support						

SOURCES

Cohn, John M., Ann L. Kelsey, and Keith Michael Fiels. *Planning for Automation: A How-To-Do-It Manual for Librarians.* 2nd ed. New York: Neal-Schuman, 1997.
Chapter 3 includes a section on Putting a Price Tag on Your Technology Plan.

Fisher, Christine. "Evolving Technology and Law Library Planning." *St. John's Law Review* 70, no. 1/2 (1996): 181–87.
This article discusses technology planning and implementation in a law library setting with emphasis on staffing, space, and budgeting.

Mayo, Diane, and Sandra Nelson, for the Public Library Association. *Wired for the Future: Developing Your Library Technology Plan.* Chicago: American Library Association, 1999.
Chapter 4, "Selecting a Technology Infrastructure and Identifying Products and Services," and Chapter 5, "Developing and Managing the Implementation Process," offer detailed discussions on cost, implementation, and plan evaluation issues.

Penniman, David. "Strategic Planning to Avoid Bottlenecks in the Age of the Internet." *Computers in Libraries* 19, no. 1 (1999): 50–53.
This article approaches planning from the point of view that clearly defined vision and mission statements will assist libraries in coping with rapidly changing technology and help keep plans stabilized and on track during periods of rapid change.

6

Working with Your Plan

IMPLEMENTATION ISSUES

Implementation of your technology plan will encompass a number of different activities. These activities involve selecting computer hardware and specific software packages that will best allow you to achieve the goals and objectives delineated in your plan—within whatever restraints may be imposed by the budget allocated for implementation.

Requesting Information from Vendors

Comprehensive requests for proposals (RFP) or more focused requests for quotations (RFQ) are often used as a means of competitively evaluating competing hardware and software, particularly those that are more complex, such as integrated library systems or wide area networks. Your technology plan and the data upon which it is built will be most useful in creating an RFP or RFQ. This information, when incorporated into the structure of such a document, along with restrictions imposed by your organization—such as the necessity to purchase from state-approved vendors or to follow hardware/software standardization requirements—will delineate for prospective vendors "what" you wish to accomplish. The vendors' task will then be to describe in detail "how" they propose, through their products and services, to actually "do" it and at what cost.

Even for less complex purchases, some sort of competitive process is valuable as a means of evaluating and selecting the best product at the most cost effective price. A short, concise RFQ or even a request for information (RFI), i.e., asking for a description of the vendor's product based on your needs and requirements and cost data, often is the perfect solution in these cases.

Installation and Maintenance

The physical installation and maintenance of products and systems will also be part of the implementation process. The degree to which the library must assume responsibility for these tasks is to a great extent dependent on the situation that exists within the library's larger organization. Your library may benefit from the presence of information systems staff who are assigned to support your technology efforts by installing and maintaining the hardware and software that is purchased. In most cases, however, you will be expected to handle some or all of these tasks.

Installation and maintenance of systems can be very difficult and time-consuming due to the interconnection of networks both internally and externally and the increased complexity of software applications and operating systems. As a result, a portion of your RFP, RFQ, or RFI will often include a section to elicit information from potential vendors regarding the costs involved in installing their products and a description of maintenance and support options that are available after installation.

Moreover, significant facilities work may need to be done in order to accommodate the equipment you plan to purchase. This might include pulling cable, installing phone lines or Internet connections, reconfiguring space to accommodate network servers and individual workstations, and increasing electrical capability to supply the power required to run the new equipment.

Time Lines

All of these considerations will drive the implementation time line. More than likely your plan will have to be implemented in phases.

A myriad of issues, including, but not limited to, vendor equipment availability, institutional purchasing time lines, budgetary review cycles, site readiness, and introducing new services to your user population, will have an impact upon how you schedule the implementation of new or upgraded technologies.

Staffing and Training

Sufficient staffing and training of both staff and users will be an integral part of the implementation process. As electronic technology has grown in our libraries, so has the need to provide adequate levels of personnel to manage it. In many libraries, what began as a few hours of a reference librarian's time has evolved into a full-blown system librarian's position. Today, with the introduction of integrated library systems built on the Windows NT operating system, as well as other complex system and telecommunications infrastructures, libraries are confronted with the need to hire Microsoft-certified engineers—or else pay the not-inconsiderable sums involved in getting one or more persons trained as such. This may be true even if the larger organization has such staff in place, particularly if the level of support required by the library is potentially significant. Requirements for staff training must be carefully delineated and vendor responses to such requirements must be evaluated with an eye toward both comprehensiveness and cost effectiveness. In many cases, staff training will have to be obtained from multiple vendors.

Equally important is user training. This training will most often be done by library staff either one-on-one or in formal classes or instructional sessions. Particularly in the beginning, significant time and resources may have to be dedicated to the development of training programs and to assisting users in becoming familiar and comfortable with using the new technology in your library to retrieve the information they are seeking. Staff will also want to develop guidelines and help assistance, both written and online, to assist users in working with the new technology. User training may also require the development of authentication strategies so that remote users can be provided with access to resources and to training in a completely online environment. These new aspects of user training may require significant amounts of time and preparation for staff during the implementation process.

ONGOING REVIEW AND EVALUATION

One of your plan's goals will be ongoing monitoring and evaluation. Technologies become obsolete, service needs change. To ensure that your plan stays current, you must build in a timetable and methodology for regular evaluations, and, as necessary, revisions and adjustments. Overall long-range and strategic plans are typically subject to cyclical review. The same should be true for your technology plan. It is a good way not only of staying on top of evolving technologies, but of keeping your ear to the ground, so to speak, with your stakeholders and constituencies. Nothing is as constant as change...and nothing is as useless as a plan that speaks to yesterday's needs.

In the not-so-distant past, five-year long-range or strategic plans were considered the norm. While the goals and, often, objectives of these plans are still reasonably sustainable for a five-year period, such is not the case with technology plans. Thinking back five years in terms of technology is to return to the almost antediluvian period when the World Wide Web was an academic oddity. Who can imagine what types of technology will be commonplace five years from now? In this time of rapid and continuous change, a technology plan covering a 24-month period is the optimum. While it is important for all plans to undergo annual evaluations and reviews, this is even more critical for technology plans. In fact, review will be almost continuous.

What will change is not the underlying foundation of the plan. The goals and objectives that focus on services to users and increased user satisfaction will remain relatively stable. Rather, what will change are the specific solutions selected to attain these objectives.

KEEPING YOUR PLAN CURRENT

Technological tools of all kinds—computers, databases, database content, multimedia resources, and telecommunications—change almost daily. While specific activities chosen to implement objectives have always been the most mutable segments of a plan, in the case of a technology plan, it is almost a given that these will change constantly. It is critical not to lose sight of the underlying premises behind these action items and to re-evaluate them constantly. For example, an important database may become available online or the price of memory may drop so that it is possible to double the amount of RAM in a workstation. Do not become so focused on the specific action item that the objective is lost sight of and outdated or less valuable services are purchased when better choices are newly available.

Midpoint Review

In addition to the ongoing review of specific action items and technological solutions, a midpoint evaluation is a valuable method of determining how well the plan is working, and what needs to be done to complete the plan. This is the time to utilize the quantitative measures built into the plan to assess whether the planned and implemented technological services and applications are achieving the goals and objectives of the plan and meeting the needs of the institution and its users. Moreover, this is a good time to assess what emerging technologies may soon offer better solutions than those currently in place and what upgrade options may be possible.

By the end of the second year, the process will have come full circle and the full planning process will begin anew. This will be true even if the organization's strategic plan is a five-year one, for it is at this time that objectives are often revised. It has been traditional to convene planning committees for specific periods of time to create a plan and then evaluate it at regular (usually annual) intervals; however, the need to constantly review and update a technology plan may require a different methodology. Perhaps the technology planning committee will be permanent, remaining knowledgeable and up-to-date about technological changes and enhancements and meeting regularly to evaluate and assess the library's service plan and the needs of different areas within the library. Membership on the committee might be rotational, with new members appointed on an annual, but staggered, basis, so that there are always members with history and experience remaining on the committee.

Whatever approach a library takes, library administration must always be cognizant of the fact that technology is ever-changing and that technological solutions incorporated within the plan must be constantly assessed and reviewed; however, it must also be careful to remain aware of the underlying foundation of the plan, the goals and objectives that form the crux of the plan for service, so that technology enables the service plan but does not drive it.

7

What Makes a Good—
and a Not So Good—
Technology Plan?

GOOD PLANS

The two most basic criteria for a good plan are obvious: First, was it implemented? Did it help you to secure the resources you needed? Did it provide sufficient direction to select, acquire, and successfully install the technological improvements outlined in the plan? Second, did it produce the intended improvements in library service? Did it make a difference for your users?

Beyond these obvious criteria, a good plan also has a number of other characteristics:

- It explains not only what you are proposing, but *why* you are proposing it.

- It is written from the perspective of library users and clearly driven by the users' needs. This is why the needs assessment part of your planning process will make a difference. It may be that you already know what the library needs, but only users can give you truly concrete examples of *why* the library needs it!

- It clearly relates to the library's mission and/or the parent organization's mission. A library cannot develop a successful technology plan without already having a long-range service plan.

- It has an immediately obvious logical progression and structure. A good plan almost "opens up" in your hand. Formatting and layout are especially important when most people reviewing the plan *will not* read the plan from cover to cover. Identifying and locating each section should be a transparent process.

- It should read like a good story. It should be readable by the average library user, which could mean the proverbial "man-in-the-street," a university researcher, corporate CFO, superintendent, municipal official, or legislator. It is always important to take your final draft to someone whose writing ability and opinion you value—and then listen to what they tell you!

- It is modular in structure. For those who developed the plan, it is easier to update or pull individual modules, and easier to mount and utilize on a Web site. The use of modules makes a plan easier to read, easier for the reader who needs to skip, or skip to, a section. For the reader, it is easier to locate information in a series of logically organized and clearly titled short documents than in a 25-page narrative!

- It provides all the information (not necessarily in excruciating detail) that a reader needs to understand the library—its users needs and proposed activities.

BAD PLANS

And a bad plan? The answer is obvious: a bad plan is either not implemented, does not get you the resources you need to implement it, or does not produce any real impact on your users.

A bad plan:

- Does not explain why you want or need equipment and services;

- Does not relate to the library's mission;

- Does not relate what you are trying to do to the needs of users;

- Does not have a logical structure and flow; and

- Does not present all the information a reader needs. (It is surprising how many plans do not even indicate what state—as in location, not condition—the library is in!)

Such a plan is probably also a poorly formatted, rambling laundry list of technical jargon so poorly organized that it is impossible to find something in it again ten minutes after you put it down!

Because of the huge number of libraries undertaking their first plan, the speed with which many organizations have developed their plans, and the tendency to leave planning to the "technical people," there really are plenty of plans out there like this. Regrettably, given the rush to purchase technology, many such plans have even been funded.

Luckily, your plan will be wonderful! After all, you have worked with your users and have this book and some good examples to guide you.

SOURCE

Rux, Paul. "Three Fatal Flaws in Planning Information Technology." *Technology Connection* 2, no. 8 (December 1995): 5, 31.
This short, but interesting article discusses flaws in the planning process that can be detrimental to information technology projects. While aimed at school media and technology specialists, it is applicable to librarians embarking on technology planning in other types of libraries as well.

Conclusion

Uses of a Technology Plan

Your library's technology plan is not really about technology. Technology is not a goal or an objective. It is a tool that enables you to provide better service to your user community. User communities vary and each is unique in its own way, just as your library is unique. User populations may be students, the general public, employees, a mix of all of these or an even more narrowly defined subset. Moreover, your library may very likely be part of a larger institutional or corporate entity.

THE PLAN AND YOUR LIBRARY'S MISSION

A successful technology plan will grow out of and be closely connected to your library and, where appropriate, your parent organization's strategic mission, goals, and objectives. A technology plan must be a canvas of realistic and attainable services and applications selected to further the achieving of these overall service priorities. Otherwise, it will be of little use.

Consortia may also create technology plans to assist in achieving the goals and objectives of member libraries. These libraries may be made up of several subsidiaries of multinational corporations, a group of school districts, public libraries, institutions of higher education, or several different types of libraries. Consortium technology plans must also arise from the consortium's plan for service, which reflects the goals and objectives of individual members. This web of planning is frequently very beneficial, for the services and applications implemented by a consortium through its technology planning efforts may, in turn, provide the mechanism for member libraries to provide services in fulfillment of their local plans. The ability of libraries to attain this symbiotic relationship through the development of synchronized technology planning is one of the most important uses and benefits of technology plans in a consortial environment.

GETTING THE MOST OUT OF YOUR TECHNOLOGY PLAN

A technology plan interconnected to the goals and objectives of a broader planning document has several important uses:

- It allows the library to position itself to take advantage of funding and other opportunities as they arise. A comprehensive technology plan, which includes an inventory of current services and applications in place as well as being a plan for extending and enhancing those services and/or adding new ones, will position a library to respond immediately when an opportunity presents itself.

- It fulfills objectives utilizing current technology, but at the same time serves as a road map for growth and development as services, applications, and technology continue to evolve.

- It answers the question "Why do you need these computers?" by specifying and emphasizing what services to users will be enhanced by acquiring specific technologies.

- It provides a venue for surveying technology in the broadest sense as a means of more effectively attaining service goals and objectives rather than focusing on networks, cabling, and computers.

- It provides a framework for staff development and user education. Using technology to further service objectives often requires a learning curve on the part of librarians, staff, and the library's user communities. Addressing these needs within the plan is a critical dimension of overall technology planning.

The uses previously described are really very generic and will apply to any type of library; however, each library must decide how these uses will be applied in its specific environment. For example, schools, colleges, and universities will focus on uses related to curriculum needs. Public libraries may emphasize access to general information and current topics and titles. Corporate libraries may concentrate on business intelligence and time-sensitive data.

What is important though is to concentrate not on the nuts and bolts of technology per se, but on the services that it can help the library to expand and enhance. This, in the end, is the primary use of a technology plan—to put together a comprehensive document that focuses on services and applications enabled by technology to advance the mission of the library and its parent organization and/ or consortial partners.

Appendix A

Technology Planning Resources on the World Wide Web: A Webliography

INTRODUCTION

The World Wide Web contains an array of sources and materials that will be of great help to anyone writing or updating a technology plan for their library. Many state libraries have created excellent, in-depth Web sites with planning tips and hints, as well as links to sample plans. Other sites focus on specific types of libraries or particular aspects of plan writing. The Web site links listed here, some of which are included in the Sources sections of the narrative, were active as of the date of access included with the annotation. This Webliography is duplicated on the accompanying CD-ROM with active links to the listed Web sites. Access to the sites requires a dial-up or direct connection to the Internet and the World Wide Web.

GENERAL RESOURCES

Integrated Library System Report [ed.]. *Technology Plans*. 1999, January 19—last update.

www.ilsr.com/sample.htm (Accessed 10 June 1999)
This electronic journal provides links to several useful technology planning guides and to sample plans created by academic, public, school, and special libraries. Included also are links to state and county library plans.

LibraryLand: Electronic Resources [ed.]. *Technology Planning.* 1999, March 27—last update.
sunsite.berkeley.edu/LibraryLand/elres/plan.htm (Accessed 10 June 1999)
This Web site provides links to technology planning guides and tip sheets and to sample public library technology plans.

National Center for Technology Planning. 1999, 4 May—last update.
www.nctp.com/ (Accessed 10 June 1999)
This comprehensive site is especially helpful for those writing plans for K–12 school districts and higher education. Lists of relevant publications, both books and articles, and links to state, district, building-level, and higher education technology plans are included.

Northwest Educational Technology Curriculum (NETC). *Technology Planning.* 1998, July 28—last update.
www.netc.org/tech_plans/ (Accessed 10 June 1999)
This site includes frequently asked questions regarding technology planning, a section on acceptable use policies, a resource list of bibliographies and publications, and sample plans from Northwest schools, districts, and states.

ACADEMIC AND SPECIAL LIBRARIES

EDUCAUSE Information Resources Library.
www.educause.edu/ir/ir-library.html (Accessed 10 June 1999)
The EDUCAUSE Information Resources Library is a comprehensive digital collection of information about managing and using information resources in higher education. The library includes papers discussing technology planning, as well as sample plans from a variety of types of academic institutions.

Hulser, Richard P. "Integrating Technology Into Strategic Planning." Special Libraries Association. *www.sla.org/pubs/serial/io/1998/feb98/hulser.html* (Accessed 10 June 1999)
This article by Richard Hulser was originally published in the February 1998 issue of *Information Outlook*. It addresses technology planning within the context of strategic planning for information services in corporate and other specialized libraries.

Kobulnicky, Paul J. "Critical Factors in Academic IT Planning." EDUCAUSE Information Resources Library. *www.educause.edu/ir/library/html/cnc9833/cnc9833.html* (Accessed 10 June 1999)
This paper, presented at CAUSE 98, discusses the technology planning process in an academic institution and its role within the larger context of the academic mission. The author views technology planning as a strategy towards achieving a larger vision rather than an objective in and of itself.

Ringle, Martin, and Daniel Updegrove. "Is Strategic Planning for Technology an Oxymoron?" EDUCAUSE Information Resources Library. *www.educause.edu/ir/library/html/cem9814.html* (Accessed 10 June 1999)
This paper, originally published in *Cause/Effect*, volume 21, number 1, 1998, presents an overview of technology planning in an academic environment. It discusses the purposes of technology planning, suggests why strategic technology planning sometimes fails, and offers suggestions for a successful outcome.

Special Libraries Association [ed.]. *Selected References on Strategic Planning*. 1999, March 15—last update. *www.sla.org/membership/irc/libstrat.html* (Accessed 10 June 1999)
This bibliography includes articles, monographs, and links to sample strategic plans and mission statements in special libraries and library associations. Although the emphasis is on strategic planning in general, technology planning as part of the strategic planning process is covered in several of the cited materials. Many of the citations have links directly to the full-text article.

PUBLIC AND SCHOOL LIBRARIES

(Includes state library and department of education sites.)

Bodolay, Sylvia. *Exemplary School Technology Plans.*
  http://projects.scrtec.org/~techplan/index.html (Accessed 10 June 1999)
  This Web page, located on the South Central Regional Technology in Education Consortium Web site, is the result of a master's thesis on technology planning. It includes a matrix to identify exemplary school plans. The elements common to exemplary plans identified through the matrix have been compiled into two on-line documents, "Technology Planning Guide" and "Tips for Technology Planning."

Connecticut State Library [ed.]. *Technology Plan Guide.* 1999, June 10—last update.
  www.cslnet.ctstateu.edu/techpln.htm (Accessed 10 June 1999)
  This site outlines the elements of a technology plan and includes a technology plan template.

Denver Public Schools [ed.]. *Technology Plan Builder.* 1999, April 19—last update.
  http://edtech.denver.k12.co.us/planner/default.html (Accessed 10 June 1999)
  This comprehensive, in-depth site, while directed at K–12 schools, has a wide array of solid information and links to other resources that will benefit planners in all types of libraries.

Illinois State Board of Education. Area 2 Learning Technologies [ed.]. *Sample Components of [a] Technology Plan.*
  www.lth2.k12.il.us/technolo.html (Accessed 10 June 1999)
  This is a fairly detailed sample technology plan designed for use by K–12 school districts.

Kansas State Department of Education [ed.]. *Technology Plans.* 1999, January 19—last update.
  www.ksbe.state.ks.us/commiss/techplans.html (Accessed 10 June 1999)
  This site, in addition to sample plans for K–12 school districts, includes links to other resources on the national level, as well as bibliographies, a glossary, and a reference list.

National Center for Super Computer Applications (NCSA) [ed.].
Building the 21st Century School.
www.ncsa.uiuc.edu/idt/ (Accessed 10 June 1999)
This site, created by the National Center for Super Computer Applications (NCSA), the North Central Regional Technology in Education Consortium (NCRTEC), and the Integrated Technology Education Group (ITEG), is intended as a decision support tool for school technology and facilities. It offers a systems approach to the planning process with flow charts, planning tables, and spreadsheets. Also included are multidimensional models of the technology-rich classroom using virtual reality modeling language (VRML).

Ryan, Joe. *Library Technology Plans by State.*
web.syr.edu/~jryan/infopro/techplan.html (Accessed 10 June 1999)
This component of a comprehensive Web site devoted to resources for information professionals provides links to technology plans arranged alphabetically by state. It also includes a How to Write a Plan section and a bibliography of guides and online resources.

Schools and Libraries Corporation [ed.]. *Technology Plans.* 1999, April 15—last update.
www.sl.universalservice.org/reference/techplans.asp (Accessed 10 June 1999)
This is the official Web site of the Schools and Libraries Division (SLD) of the Universal Service Administrative Company (USAC). An explanation of SLD's technology plan policies and procedures with accompanying frequently asked questions is included in the Reference area of the Web site. This will be of special interest to public and school libraries filling out E-rate applications.

State Library of Florida. Florida Department of State [ed.]. *Technology Planning Made Easy.* 1998, July 29—last update.
http://dlis.dos.state.fl.us/e-rate/techplan/tech_plan.htm (Accessed 10 June 1999)
This basic guide, directed toward public libraries, emphasizes developing plans to meet the requirements of the Schools and Libraries Division for participation in the Federal Universal Service Fund program. The guide is available as both a Microsoft Word and a PDF document. These formats require that Microsoft Word 97 or Adobe Acrobat viewer software be installed on the reader's

computer. A number of other resources, as well as links to sample plans are also on this Web site.

State of Wisconsin. Wisconsin Department of Public Instruction. Public Library Development. *Library Technology Planning.* 1998, March 20—last updated.
www.dpi.state.wi.us/dlcl/pld/planout.html (Accessed 10 June 1999)
This site focuses on technology planning information and resources for public libraries. Included are factors to be considered when developing a technology plan, sample plans, and an excellent planning resources section with links to E-rate plan criteria, other plans, and planning resources available at other agencies. This site is an excellent gateway particularly for public libraries.

U.S. Department of Education. Office of Educational Technology [ed.]. *State Technology Web Sites and Contacts.* 1999, 12 March—last update.
www.ed.gov/Technology/sta_tech.html (Accessed 10 June 1999)
This site lists contact names, addresses, phone numbers, and e-mail addresses of state technology officers and offices, as well as state technology plans.

Washington State Educational Technology Support Center [ed.]. *Sample Technology Plan Page.* 1997, November 7—last update.
www.esd105.wednet.edu/techplan.html (Accessed 10 June 1999)
This site provides a detailed, comprehensive checklist for the preparation of technology plans for Universal Service Fund (E-rate) applications and to fulfill requirements for fully developed technology plans for K–12 school districts. The checklist requires that Adobe Acrobat viewer software be loaded on the reader's computer.

Appendix B

About the CD-ROM

The CD-ROM accompanying this book describes the material on the CD-ROM and how to use it, fifty technology plans collected from different types of libraries, and a Webliography based on the Webliography in Appendix A, "Technology Planning Resources on the World Wide Web: A Webliography." The CD-ROM is a Web page accessible through the standard Internet browsers, Netscape or Internet Explorer. It is best viewed using the most recent versions of each browser.

To begin, insert the CD-ROM in the CD-ROM drive of your computer, activate your browser, click on "File" on the tool bar, and select the "Open" option. Access the drive that your CD-ROM is located in and click on the "TechPlan_toc" file to open it. The "Technology Plans Web Page" table of contents will display.

Click on "About the CD-ROM" to display this text for easy reference as you navigate the Web page.

Click on "Technology Plans" to search for and display the plans themselves.

The plans are searchable by type of library and by library name. All links within the plans are internally accessible on the CD-ROM and require no outside connection to the Internet. To achieve this, links within each plan to external Web sites are not active, but the addresses remain in the text for your use and reference.

Academic and research, public, school, and special libraries developed these fifty plans. They illustrate many of the points made in the text and enable the reader to easily examine the complete texts of plans referred to specifically in the narrative, as well as to study plans from many other libraries. The plans are included as models to help you make the best use of existing concepts and language in creating your library's own unique technology plan.

Click on "Technology Planning Resources on the World Wide Web: A Webliography," to display the Webliography. The links are active links to the listed Web sites. Access to the sites requires a dial-up or direct connection to the Internet and the World Wide Web.

ALPHABETICAL LIST OF LIBRARIES CONTRIBUTING PLANS

Altoona Area Public Library, Altoona, Pennsylvania
Avon Free Public Library, Avon, Connecticut
Batesville Memorial Library, Batesville, Indiana
Buffalo and Erie County Public Library, Buffalo, New York
Bureau of Indian Affairs, Office of Indian Education Program, Washington, D.C.
Burlington County Library System, Westhampton, New Jersey
Cabrillo College, Robert E. Swenson Library, Aptos, California
Coastal Carolina University, Conway, South Carolina
Colorado Alliance of Research Libraries, Denver, Colorado
County College of Morris, Randolph, New Jersey
Decatur City Schools, Decatur, Alabama
Delaware County Library System, Media, Pennsylvania
Denver Public Schools, Denver, Colorado
Derby Neck Library, Derby, Connecticut
Fall Mountain Regional School District, Langdon, New Hampshire
Finger Lakes Library System, Ithaca, New York
Hingham Public Library, Hingham, Massachusetts
Hoover Public Library, Hoover, Alabama
Indiana State University, Terre Haute, Indiana
Kansas City Public Library, Kansas City, Missouri
Kitsap Regional Library, Bremerton, Washington
Lake County Public Library, Merrillville, Indiana
Marlborough Public Library, Marlborough, Massachusetts
McMillan Memorial Library, Wisconsin Rapids, Wisconsin
Monroe Public Library, Monroe, Connecticut
Montclair Public Library, Montclair, New Jersey
Naval Research Laboratory, Ruth H. Hooker Research Library and Technical Information Center, Washington, D.C.

New Mexico State University, Las Cruces, New Mexico

New York State Appellate Division Law Library, Fourth Department, Rochester, New York

New York State Comprehensive Research Libraries Group

Newton Falls Public Library, Newton Falls, Ohio

Ridgeview Elementary School, Yucaipa-Calimesa Joint Unified School District, Yucaipa, California

Rochester Hills Public Library, Rochester, Michigan

Russell Library, Middletown, Connecticut

Sturgis Library, Barnstable, Massachusetts

T. B. Scott Free Library, Merrill, Wisconsin

Tampa Bay Library Consortium, Tampa, Florida

Tippecanoe County Public Library, Lafayette, Indiana

United States Army Corps of Engineers (USACE) Library Program, Vicksburg, Mississippi

University of California, Berkeley, Media Resources Center, Multimedia Server Project, Berkeley, California

University of Florida, Health Science Center Libraries, Gainesville, Florida

University of Pittsburgh, University Library System, Pittsburgh, Pennsylvania

University of Southern Maine, Portland, Maine

University of Tennessee, Knoxville, Knoxville, Tennessee

University of Wisconsin, Oshkosh, Oshkosh, Wisconsin

Urbana Free Public Library, Urbana, Illinois

Vandergrift Public Library, Vandergrift, Pennsylvania

Vineland Public Library, Vineland, New Jersey

Washington University, St. Louis, Missouri

West Orange Public Library, West Orange, New Jersey

Appendix C

List of Library Technology Plans on the CD-ROM

ACADEMIC AND RESEARCH LIBRARIES

Cabrillo College, Robert E, Swenson Library, Aptos, California, 1/99

Cabrillo College, Robert E, Swenson Library, Aptos, California, 6/99

Coastal Carolina University, Conway, South Carolina

Colorado Alliance of Research Libraries, Denver, Colorado

County College of Morris, Randolph, New Jersey

Indiana State University, Terre Haute, Indiana

New Mexico State University, Las Cruces, New Mexico

New York State Comprehensive Research Libraries Group

University of Pittsburgh, University Library System, Pittsburgh, Pennsylvania

University of Southern Maine, Portland, Maine

University of Tennessee, Knoxville, Knoxville, Tennessee

University, of Wisconsin, Oshkosh, Oshkosh, Wisconsin (1997 Plan)

University of Wisconsin, Oshkosh, Oshkosh, Wisconsin (1999 Update)

Washington University, St, Louis, Missouri

PUBLIC LIBRARIES

Altoona Area Public Library, Altoona, Pennsylvania
Avon Free Public Library, Avon, Connecticut
Batesville Memorial Library, Batesville, Indiana
Buffalo and Erie County Public Library, Buffalo, New York
Burlington County Library System, Westhampton, New Jersey
Delaware County Public Library System, Media, Pennsylvania
Derby Neck Library, Derby, Connecticut
Finger Lakes Library System, Ithaca, New York
Hingham Public Library, Hingham, Massachusetts
Hoover Public Library, Hoover, Alabama
Kansas City Public Library, Kansas City, Missouri
Kitsap Regional Library, Bremerton, Washington
Lake County Public Library, Merrillville, Indiana
Marlborough Public Library, Marlborough, Massachusetts
McMillan Memorial Library, Wisconsin Rapids, Wisconsin
Monroe Public Library, Monroe, Connecticut
Montclair Public Library, Montclair, New Jersey
Newton Falls Public Library, Newton Falls, Ohio
Rochester Hills Public Library, Rochester, Michigan
Russell Library, Middletown, Connecticut
Sturgis Library, Barnstable, Massachusetts
T. B. Scott Free Library, Merrill, Wisconsin
Tampa Bay Library Consortium, Tampa, Florida (Multi-type Library Consortium)
Tippecanoe County Public Library, Lafayette, Indiana
Urbana Free Public Library, Urbana, Illinois
Vandergrift Public Library, Vandergrift, Pennsylvania
Vineland Public Library, Vineland, New Jersey
West Orange Public Library, West Orange, New Jersey

SCHOOL LIBRARIES

Decatur City Schools, Decatur, Alabama
Denver Public Schools, Denver, Colorado
Fall Mountain Regional School District, Langdon, New Hampshire
Ridgeview Elementary School, Yucaipa-Calimesa Joint Unified School District, Yucaipa, California

SPECIAL LIBRARIES

Bureau of Indian Affairs, Office of Indian Education Program, Washington, D.C.

Naval Research Laboratory, Ruth H. Hooker Research Library and Technical Information Center, Washington, D.C.

New York State Appellate Division Law Library, Fourth Department, Rochester, New York

United States Army Corps of Engineers (USACE) Library Program, Vicksburg, Mississippi

University of California, Berkeley, Media Resources Center, Multimedia Server Project, Berkeley, California

University of Florida, Health Science Center Libraries, Gainesville, Florida

NOTES / CREDITS

Altoona Area Public Library, Altoona, Pennsylvania
- Altoona Area Public Library

Avon Free Public Library, Avon, Connecticut
- This plan was developed by the Management Team of the Avon Free Public Library with thanks to the Technology Committee of the Avon Library Board and Technology Plans of many public libraries who have gone before us.

Batesville Memorial Library, Batesville, Indiana
- Batesville Memorial Public Library, Batesville, Indiana Michael J. Kruse, Director

Buffalo and Erie County Public Library, Buffalo, New York
- Technology Plan of the Buffalo and Erie County Public Library

Cabrillo College, Robert E. Swenson Library, Aptos, California
- Johanna E. Bowen, Cabrillo College Library Director

Coastal Carolina University, Conway, South Carolina
- Peter Balsamo, Robin Boyea, Dave Bryon, Paul Camp, Charles Gidney, Marvin Marozas, David Parker, Debbie Stanley, Charmaine Tomczyk, Abdallah Haddad, Benjoe Juliano, Michael Lackey, Susan Libes

Colorado Alliance of Research Libraries, Denver, Colorado
* Colorado Alliance of Research Libraries

County College of Morris, Randolph, New Jersey
* County College of Morris

Delaware County Public Library System, Media, Pennsylvania
* Reprinted with permission of the Delaware County Library System, Media, PA 19063

Denver Public Schools, Denver, Colorado
* Copyright 1998 Denver Public Schools, Denver, Colorado

Derby Neck Library, Derby, Connecticut
* This plan was written by Judith Wood Augusta, Head Librarian, and approved by the Board of Directors, Derby Neck Library, Derby, Connecticut.

Fall Mountain Regional School District, Langdon, New Hampshire
* This plan was developed by the Fall Mountain Regional School District Technology Committee.

Finger Lakes Library System, Ithaca, New York
* This plan was developed by The Finger Lakes Library System.

Hoover Public Library, Hoover, Alabama
* Hoover Public Library's Technology Plan was developed by Patricia H, Guarino, Systems Specialist—Hoover Public Library (Alabama).

Indiana State University, Terre Haute, Indiana
* Strategic Planning Team, Cunningham Memorial Library, Indiana State University

Kansas City Public Library, Kansas City, Missouri
* Kansas City Public Library, Kansas City, Missouri

Lake County Public Library, Merrillville, Indiana
* Developed by the Lake County Public Library, Merrillville, Indiana

Marlborough Public Library, Marlborough, Massachusetts
* Karen Tobin, Assistant Director

McMillan Memorial Library, Wisconsin Rapids, Wisconsin
* McMillan Library, Wisconsin Rapids, Wisconsin

Monroe Public Library, Monroe, Connecticut
* The Technology Plan for the Monroe Public Library, Monroe, Connecticut was written by the Library Director, Lynne M. Rosato and approved by the Library Board of Directors.

Montclair Public Library, Montclair, New Jersey
* Courtesy of The Montclair Public Library

New Mexico State University, Las Cruces, New Mexico
* Provided by New Mexico State University, www.rumsu.edu

New York State Appellate Division Law Library, Fourth Department, Rochester, New York
* Prepared for the NY Supreme Court, Appellate Division Law Library, Fourth Department by Stephen P. Weitzer, Senior Law Librarian.

New York State Comprehensive Research Libraries Group
* This plan was produced on behalf of the New York Comprehensive Research Libraries Group; Nancy Kranich, Convener and Leslie Burger, Consultant, with funds from the Andrew W. Mellon Foundation.

Ridgeview Elementary School, Yucaipa-Calimesa Joint Unified School District, Yucaipa, California
* Ridgeview Elementary School Technology Plan developed by Paul Jessup, Tom Dryer, Tom Slider, Suzann Smith, and implemented by RES staff.

Rochester Hills Public Library, Rochester Michigan
* Larry P. Neal, Rochester Hills Public Library/ Clinton-Macomb Public Library (Mich.)

Russell Library, Middletown, Connecticut
* Russell Library, Middletown, Connecticut

Sturgis Library, Barnstable, Massachusetts
* Sturgis Library, Barnstable

Tampa Bay Library Consortium, Tampa, Florida
- Tampa Bay Library Consortium, Inc.

T.B. Scott Free Library, Merrill, Wisconsin
- T.B. Scott Free Library—Merrill, Wisconsin

Tippecanoe County Public Library, Lafayette, Indiana
- Copyright, Tippecanoe County Public Library, Lafayette, Indiana

University of California, Berkeley, Media Resources Center, Multimedia Server Project, Berkeley, California
- Gary Handman Director, Media Resources Center, UC Berkeley

University of Florida, Health Science Center Libraries, Gainesville, Florida
- University of Florida Health Science Center Library Staff

University of Southern Maine, Portland, Maine
- Copyright 1998; University of Southern Maine

University of Tennessee, Knoxville, Knoxville, Tennessee
- University Libraries, University of Tennessee, Knoxville

University of Wisconsin, Oshkosh, Oshkosh, Wisconsin
- Forest R. Polk Library, Information Technology Division, University of Wisconsin, Oshkosh

Urbana Free Public Library, Urbana, Illinois
- Courtesy of the Urbana Free Library, Copyright 1997 by The Urbana Free Library

Vandergrift Public Library, Vandergrift, Pennsylvania
- Vandergrift Public Library, Vandergrift, Pennsylvania

Vineland Public Library, Vineland, New Jersey
- Vineland Public Library, Vineland, New Jersey

West Orange Public Library, West Orange, New Jersey
- West Orange Public Library Technology Plan, Rev 3/1999, West Orange Public Library, West Orange, New Jersey

Index

About the Authors

John M. Cohn and Ann L. Kelsey are Director and Associate Director respectively of the Sherman H. Masten Learning Resource Center at the County College of Morris in Randolph, New Jersey, and partners in DocuMentors, an independent consulting firm.

Keith Michael Fiels is Director of the Massachusetts Board of Library Commissioners in Boston, Massachusetts.